Table of Contents

Pan Bread Cover & Basket Ruffle, **page 18**

Sand Dunes Pillow,
page 47

Emerald Isle Place Mat,
page 24

Dancing Ribbons Place Mat
& Napkin Ring, **page 10**

House of White Birches, Berne, Indiana 46711   AnniesAttic.com

Monk's Cloth Embroidery

Monk's cloth embroidery started in northwest Europe as huck embroidery, a technique used to decorate clothing and household linens. Ladies who used this technique stitched elaborate patterns on a specialty fabric called huck or hucka-back. Huck embroidery became popular in the United States in the late 1940s when homemakers decorated the borders of colorful huck towels with embroidery floss. A loosely woven, even-weave fabric called monk's cloth is now used for huck embroidery. Monk's cloth embroidered with worsted weight yarn is also called Swedish weaving. Today, embroidered monk's cloth is used to make sofa throws, baby blankets, pillows, wall hangings, pictures, table linens and clothing. A variety of threads, yarns and ribbons can be used.

Materials

Monk's cloth: A 100 percent cotton cloth with a loose over and under four-strand weave, monk's cloth can be found at craft and fabric stores. When purchasing monk's cloth allow for 15 percent shrinkage. Zigzag-stitch the raw edges to prevent the cloth from unraveling. Wash with detergent in warm water on the delicate cycle. Dry in the dryer.

Needle: #13 yarn needle

Yarn: Worsted weight yarn is usually used. Measure the yarn for each row against the length (L) of the fabric the number of times given in the pattern and then add 8 inches. For example, 2 L + 8 inches means to use a piece of yarn twice the length of the monk's cloth plus another 8 inches. Do not stretch the yarn when measuring.

Safety pins: Use pins to mark the center point and design starting points.

Terminology

Selvage edge: the finished edge of the fabric.

Float: the four strands of thread that run vertically along monk's cloth.

Row: the boxes (four vertical and four horizontal threads) which run from top to bottom and side to side (Fig. 1).

Fig. 1

Stitching Techniques

Start from the center of the fabric, and work the design to the edge. To find the center, fold the cloth in half vertically, and then in half horizontally. Place a safety pin in the center float to mark the center of the fabric.

The charts use different colors for the rows to make it easier to follow each row's path. This is important when rows share the same floats. These chart colors are not the colors used for our photographed projects.

There is a star on some charts marking the center of each pattern. This is where the first stitch will be made at the center of the fabric.

Make the first stitch under the four vertical strands of the float without catching the horizontal strands.

The yarn should not be visible on the backside of the fabric, since the yarn lies on the top of the threads below the float.

After making the first stitch, position half of the yarn on each side of the center float (Fig. 2).

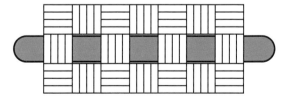

Fig. 2

Stitch from the center of each row toward the edges. When you reach the edge, remove the needle, and turn the fabric upside down. Rethread the needle with the other half of the yarn and work to the other edge. Holding a thumb over the first stitch will help the yarn glide through the float easily and keep the yarn from pulling the float out of shape.

At the end of the row, bring the yarn through to the back of the monk's cloth, leaving it on the back side. For designs that do not end at the edge of the fabric, bring the yarn back through a few floats on the front of the piece. Then bring the yarn to the back of the piece and clip it. If the selvage edge of the fabric is tightly woven at the end of the row, turn the piece around 180 degrees and follow the stitches back through the last 4 to 8 stitches on the front of the fabric. Clip remaining yarn.

Special Stitches

Step Stitch Up

Stitch a float, then bring the yarn up in the same column, and stitch a float as shown on the chart (Fig. 3).

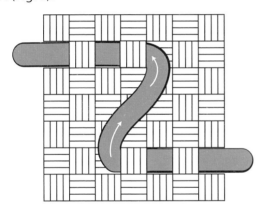

Fig. 3

Step Stitch Down

Stitch a float, and then bring the yarn down in the same column, and stitch a float as shown on the chart (Fig. 4).

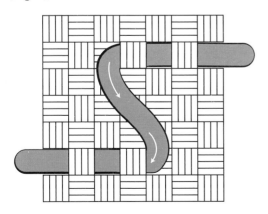

Fig. 4

Loop Stitch

Stitch a float, then turn the needle and stitch the float at the top of the loop. Turn the needle back to the correct position and re-stitch the float at the bottom of the loop (Fig. 5).

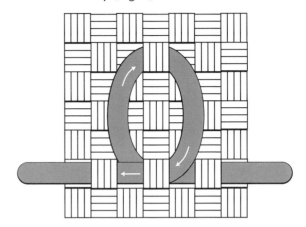

Fig. 5

Twisted Loop Stitch

Stitch a float. Keeping the needle pointing in the same direction, stitch the float at the top of the loop, then re-stitch the float at the bottom of the loop (Fig. 6).

Fig. 6

Finishing

Zigzag-stitch the raw edges of the project, leaving 4 to 24 rows for the fringe. Unravel the fringe, then fold over the selvage edges and sew.

Caring for Your Project

Wash by hand with a mild soap, and dry flat. Store in a cloth bag or in acid-free tissue paper, never in plastic. Store flat or rolled instead of folded. ❖

Flying Geese Pot Holder

Design by Jeanne Tams

Skill Level

EASY

Finished Size
10 inches square, including fringe

Materials
- Monk's cloth:
  ⅜ yd natural
- Red Heart Super Saver medium
  (7 oz/364 yds/198g per skein):
  1 skein #387 soft navy
- Tapestry needle

Pattern Notes
Every row is stitched with same color yarn. To make chart easier to read, yarn is drawn in colors, but only one color of yarn is used.

The chart colors are not the colors used in the projects.

Instructions
Yarn Length
All rows: L + 8 inches ❖

The red line is the cutting line. The blue line is the stitching line.

5

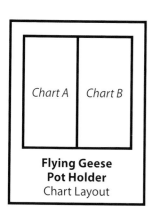

**Flying Geese
Pot Holder**
Chart Layout

Row 1

**Flying Geese
Pot Holder**
Chart A

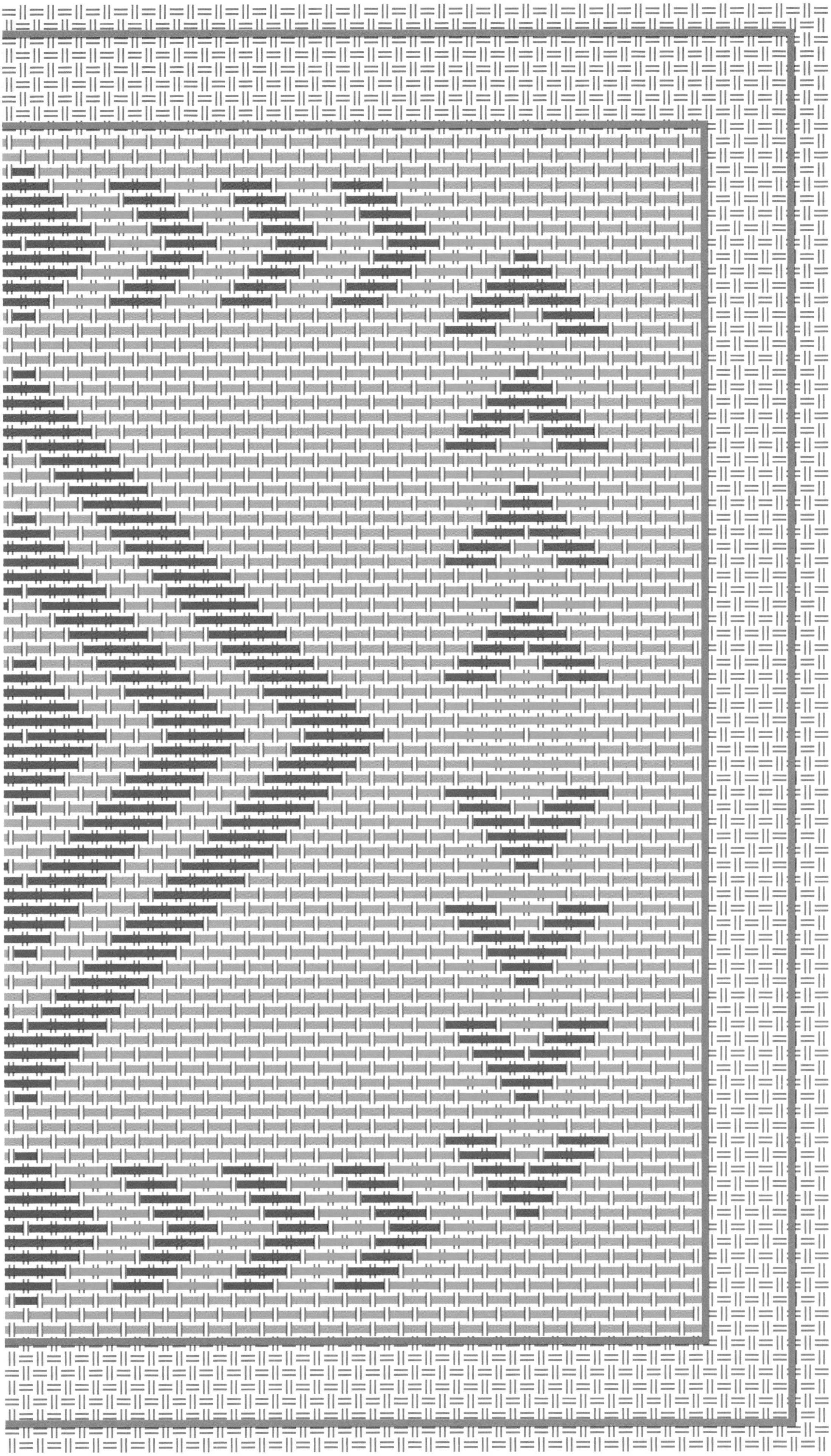

**Flying Geese
Pot Holder**
Chart B

Four-Square Pot Holder

Design by Jeanne Tams

Skill Level

EASY

Finished Size
10 inches x 10 inches

Materials
- Monk's cloth:
  ⅜ yd natural
- Red Heart Classic medium
  (3½ oz/190 yds/99g per skein):
  1 skein each #633 dark sage,
  #631 light sage and #588 amethyst
- Medium (worsted) weight yarn:
  1 oz/50 yds/56g green
- Tapestry needle

Pattern Notes
The chart colors are not the colors used in the projects.

Star marks beginning of stitching.

Instructions
Yarn Length

Rows 1–4: 18 inches

Rows 5–8: 17 inches

Rows 9–12: 16 inches

Rows 13–16: 15 inches

Rows 17–20: 14 inches

Rows 21–24: 13 inches

Rows 25–28: 12 inches

Rows 29–32: 11 inches

Rows 33–36: 10 inches

Rows 37 & 38: 9 inches ❖

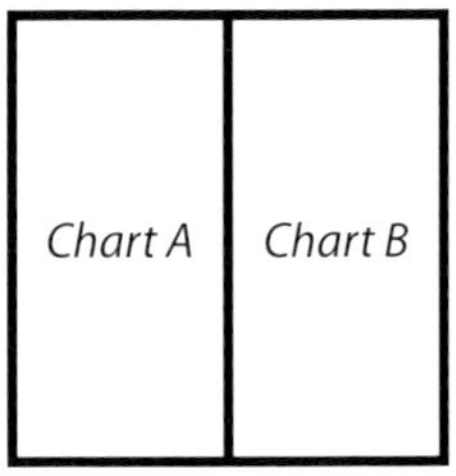

8

The red line is the cutting line. The blue line is the stitching line.

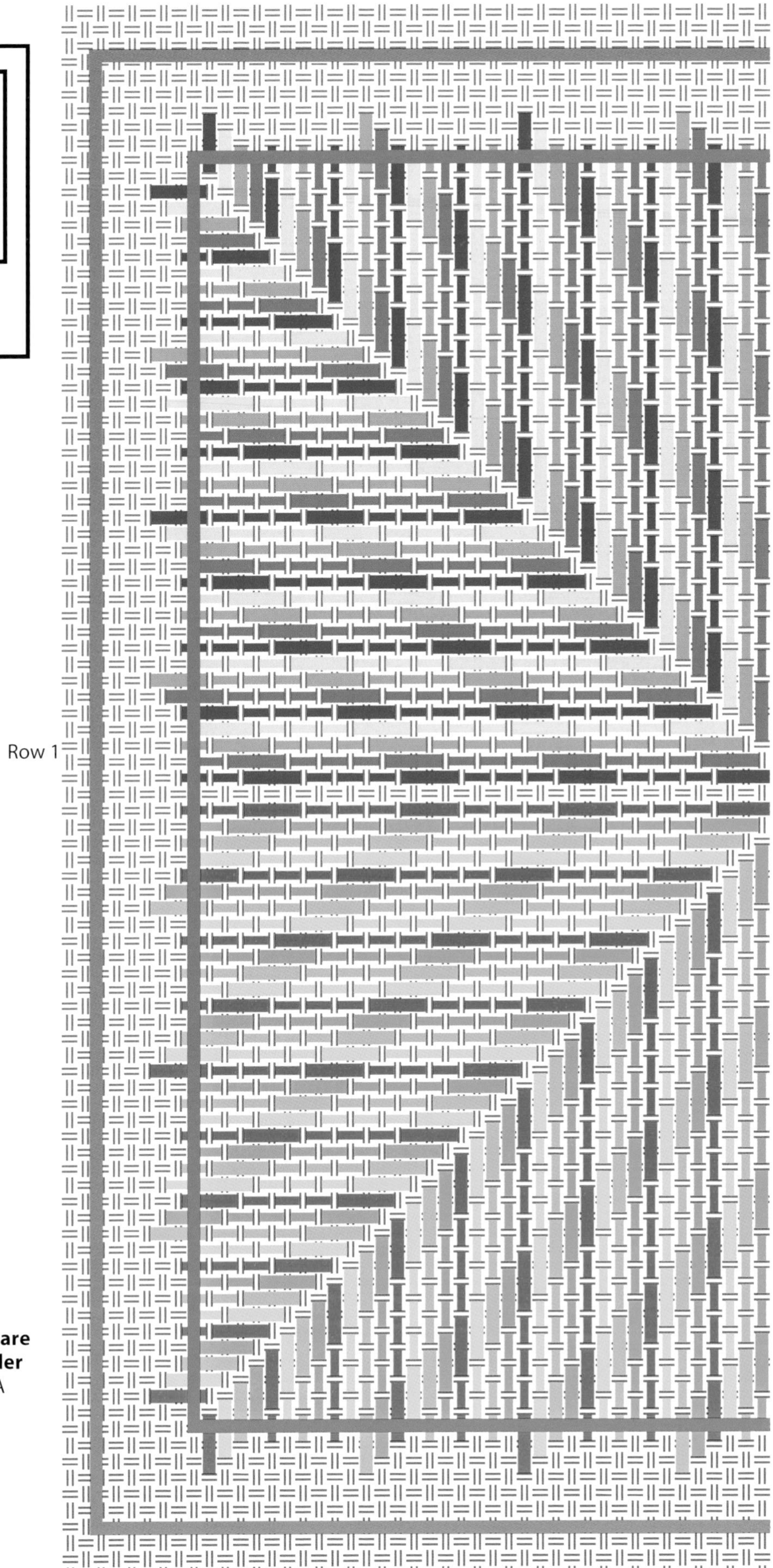

Chart A | **Chart B**

**Four-Square
Pot Holder**
Chart Layout

Row 1

**Four-Square
Pot Holder**
Chart A

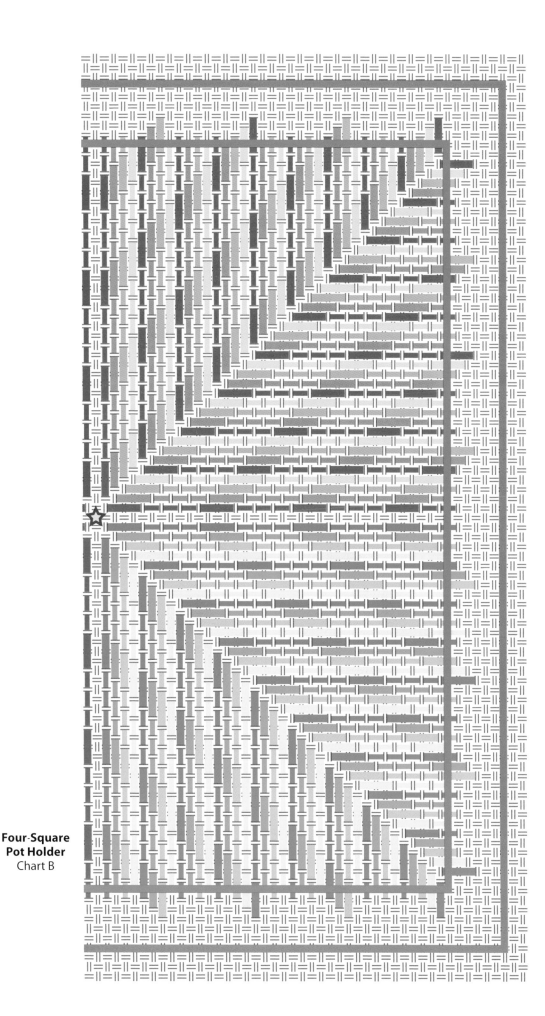

**Four-Square
Pot Holder**
Chart B

Dancing Ribbons Place Mat & Napkin Ring

Design by Jeanne Tams

Skill Level

EASY

Finished Sizes

Place Mat: 22 inches x 15½ inches, including fringe

Napkin Ring: 6½ inches x 7½ inches, including fringe

Materials

- Monk's cloth:
  ¾ yd white
- Medium (worsted) weight yarn:
  3 oz/150 yds/84g each black, light yellow, yellow, orange, red, burgundy, blue, sea green and light sea green
- Tapestry needle

4 MEDIUM

Pattern Notes

Entire stitching pattern is not shown on chart; repeat pattern across place mat.

Star marks beginning of stitching for place mat.

Instructions
Yarn Length & Color

Rows 1, 17, 27: 1½ L + 8 inches blue

Rows 2, 16, 18: 1¾ L + 8 inches black

Rows 3, 15, 19: 1¾ L + 8 inches light yellow

Rows 4, 14, 20: 2¼ L + 8 inches yellow

Rows 5, 13, 21: 2¼ L + 8 inches orange

Rows 6, 12, 22: 2½ L + 8 inches red

Rows 7, 11, 23: 2½ L + 8 inches burgundy

Rows 8, 24: 2¾ L + 8 inches green

Rows 9, 25: 2¾ L + 8 inches light sea green

Rows 10, 26, 30: 2¾ L + 8 inches sea green

Row 28: 2½ L + 8 inches sea green

Row 29: 2½ L + 8 inches light sea green

Finishing
Stay stitch ½-inch from top and bottom edges, and along side seams of Napkin Ring. Remove threads to form fringe on long sides. Sew short ends tog, leaving a ⅝-inch seam. ❖

The red line is the cutting line. The blue line is the stitching line.

Dancing Ribbons Napkin Ring
Chart

Rows
10
9
8
7
6
5
4
3
2
1
2
3
4
5
6
7
8
9
10

Rows
30
29
28
27
26
25
24
23
22
21
20
19
18
17
16
15
14
13
12
11
10
9
8
7
6
5
4
3
2
1

Dancing Ribbons Place Mat
Chart A

Dancing Ribbons Place Mat
Chart B

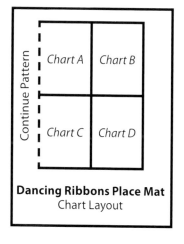

Dancing Ribbons Place Mat
Chart Layout

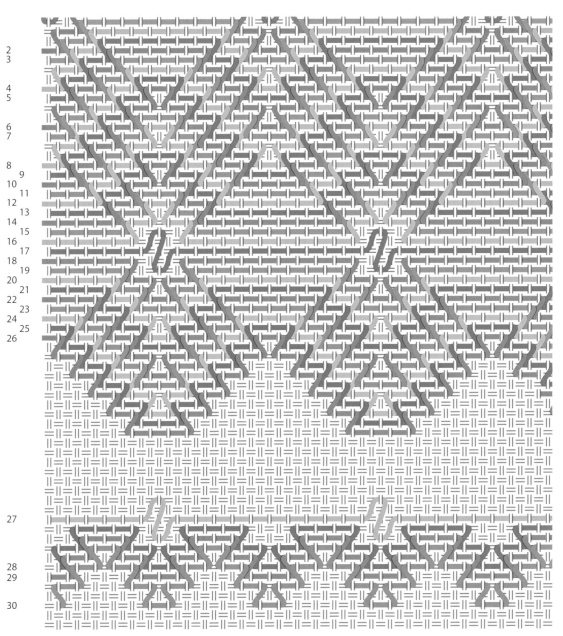

2
3
4
5
6
7
8
9
10
11
12
13
14
15
16
17
18
19
20
21
22
23
24
25
26
27
28
29
30

Dancing Ribbons Place Mat
Chart C

Dancing Ribbons Place Mat
Chart D

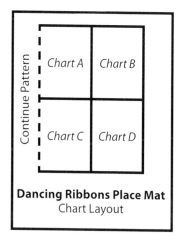

Dancing Ribbons Place Mat
Chart Layout

Checkerboard Coasters

Design by Jeanne Tams

Skill Level

■■□□
EASY

Finished Size
4½ inches x 4½ inches

Materials
• Monk's cloth:
    ¼ yd natural
• Red Heart Super Saver medium
    (7 oz/364 yds/198g per skein):
        1 skein each #633 dark sage,
        #374 country rose and #334 buff

4
MEDIUM

• Red Heart Classic medium
    (3½ oz/190 yds/99g per skein):
        1 skein #762 claret
• Tapestry needle

Pattern Notes
The chart colors are not the colors used in the projects.

Instructions
Yarn Length
All rows: 30 inches ❖

The red line is the cutting line. The blue line is the stitching line.

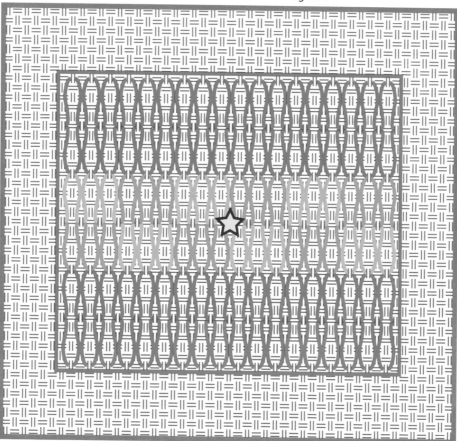

Checkerboard Coasters
Chart

Step 1

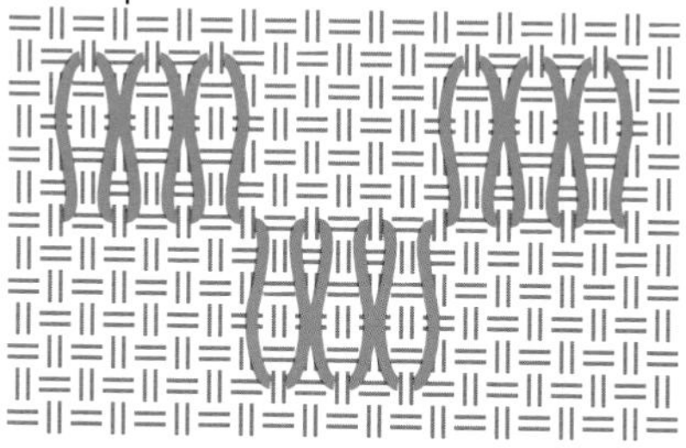

Step 2

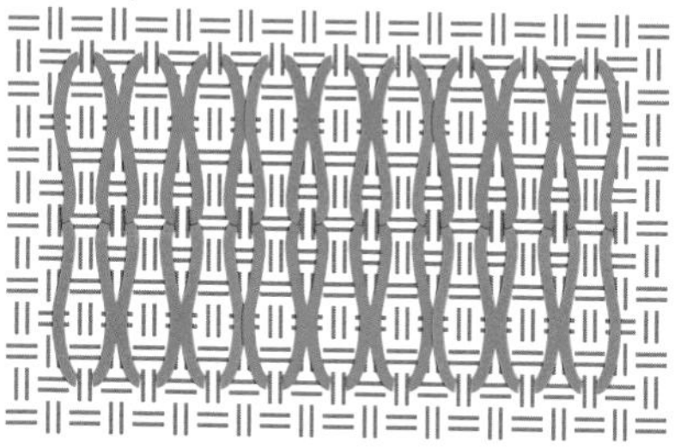

Pan Bread Cover & Basket Ruffle

Design by Jeanne Tams

Skill Level

EASY

Finished Sizes

Bread cover: 15 inches x 15 inches, including fringe

Basket ruffle: 6 inches x 62 inches, including fringe

Materials

- Monk's cloth:
  2 yds natural (or ½ yd if ruffle is pieced in 2 sections)
- Medium (worsted) weight yarn:
  2 oz/100 yds/56g each dark brown, brown, tan, blue and dark green
- Tapestry needle
- 8 inches x 11 inches x 6½ inches oval basket
- Clothespins
- Glue

Pattern Notes

Row 1: Count down 38 rows and over 68 rows to begin at edge

Rows 3–9: Twisted loop stitch

The chart colors are not the colors used in the projects.

Instructions

Bread Cover
Yarn Length & Color

Rows 1 & 2, 10: 26 inches dark brown/dark green/brown/blue

Row 3: 38 inches dark brown/dark green/brown/blue

Rows 4 & 5: 33 inches dark brown/dark green/brown/blue

Row 6: 39 inches dark brown/dark green/brown/blue

Rows 7 & 8: 32 inches dark brown/dark green/brown/blue

Row 9: 31 inches dark brown/dark green/brown/blue

Basket Ruffle
Yarn Length & Color

Rows 1, 13: 1½ L + 8 inches dark brown

Rows 2, 12: 1½ L + 8 inches brown

Rows 3 & 4, 10 & 11: 1½ L + 8 inches tan

Rows 5, 9: 1½ L + 8 inches brown

Rows 6, 8: 1½ L + 8 inches dark brown

Row 7: 2L + 8 inches blue

Finishing

Stay stitch ½-inch from top and bottom edges and along side seams of Ruffle. Remove threads to form fringe. Stitch gathering thread ½-inch from top edge of Ruffle. Sew ⅝-inch side seam. Pull gathering thread. Use clothes pins to temporarily arrange Ruffle on basket. Glue Ruffle to basket. ❖

Basket Ruffle
Chart

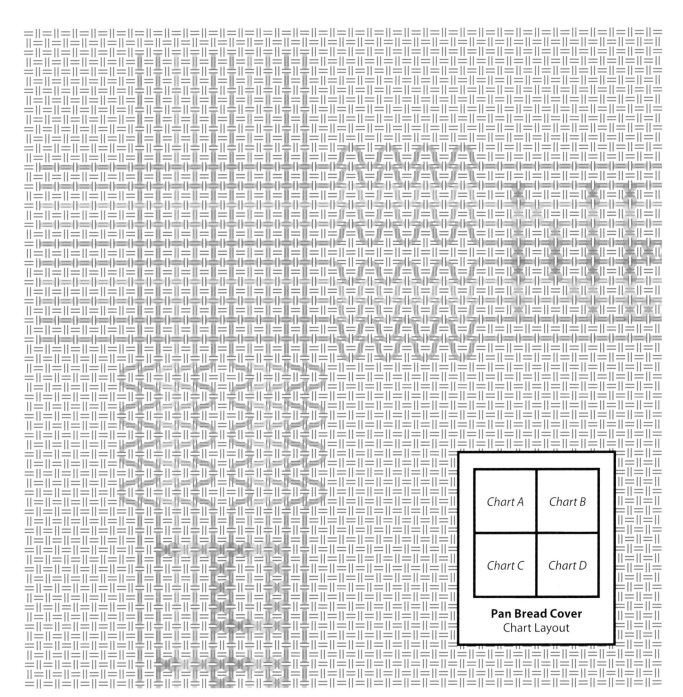

Chart A | Chart B
Chart C | Chart D

Pan Bread Cover
Chart Layout

Pan Bread Cover
Chart A

Pan Bread Cover
Chart B

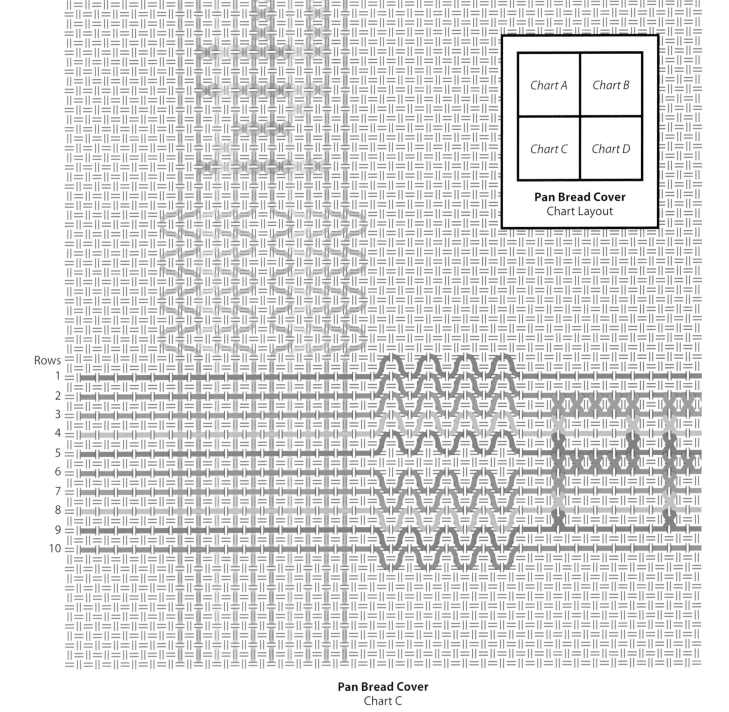

Rows

1
2
3
4
5
6
7
8
9
10

Pan Bread Cover
Chart C

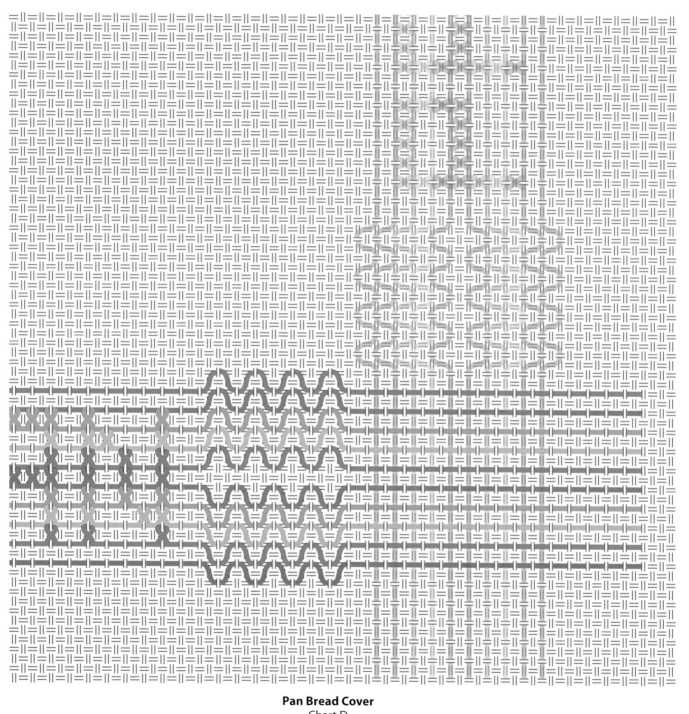

Pan Bread Cover
Chart D

Chart B	Chart D
Chart A	Chart C

**Emerald Isle
Place Mat**
Chart Layout

Emerald Isle Place Mat

Design by Jeanne Tams

Skill Level

EASY

Finished Size
16 inches x 21 inches, including fringe

Materials
- Monk's cloth:
    ⅝ yd natural
- Red Heart Super Saver medium
  (7 oz/364 yds/198g per skein):
    1 skein #633 dark sage
- Tapestry needle

**4
MEDIUM**

Pattern Notes
Every row is stitched with same color yarn. To make chart easier to read, yarn is drawn in colors, but only one color of yarn is used.

The chart colors are not the colors used in the projects.

Star marks beginning of stitching.

Instructions
Yarn Length
All rows: L + 8 inches ❖

Emerald Isle Place Mat
Chart A

Row 1

Emerald Isle Place Mat
Chart B

Emerald Isle Place Mat
Chart C

Emerald Isle Place Mat
Chart D

Fireworks Celebration

Design by Jeanne Tams

Skill Level

EASY

Finished Size
43 inches x 19½ inches

Materials
- Monk's cloth:
  ⅔ yd white
- Medium (worsted) weight yarn:
  2 oz/100 yds/56g variegated
- Tapestry needle

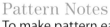

Pattern Notes
To make pattern easier to follow, the stitching on the word "Celebrate" progresses from color to color. Yarn is 1 piece. The "T" is crossed after word "Celebrate" is stitched. Secure yarn ends for word "Celebrate" and "Fireworks" on backside of fabric or retrace 6–8 floats on front side and clip.

Star marks beginning of stitching.

Instructions
Yarn Length
Fireworks: 18 inches

Celebrate: 56 inches

Confetti at end: 1¾ L + 8 inches ❖

House of White Birches, Berne, Indiana 46711   AnniesAttic.com

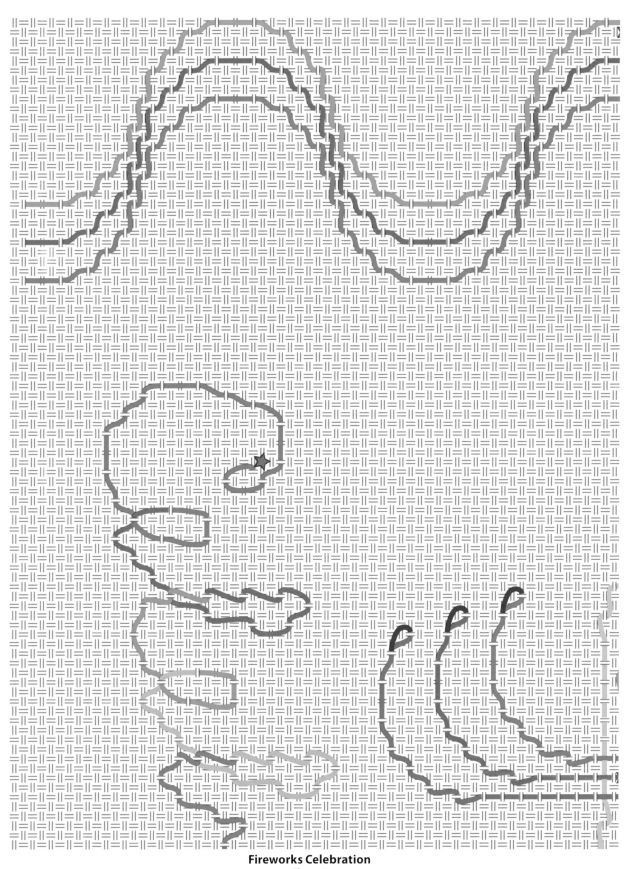

Fireworks Celebration
Chart A

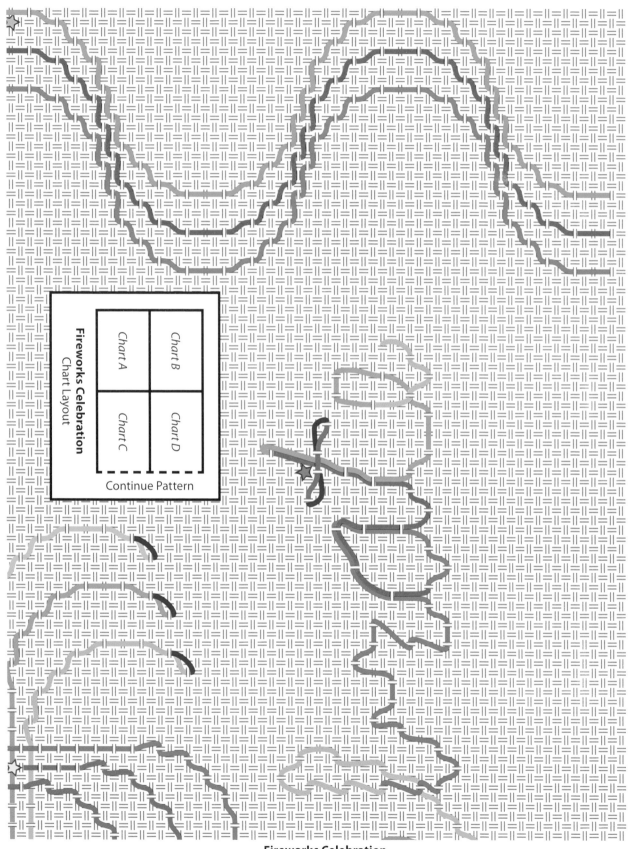

Fireworks Celebration
Chart B

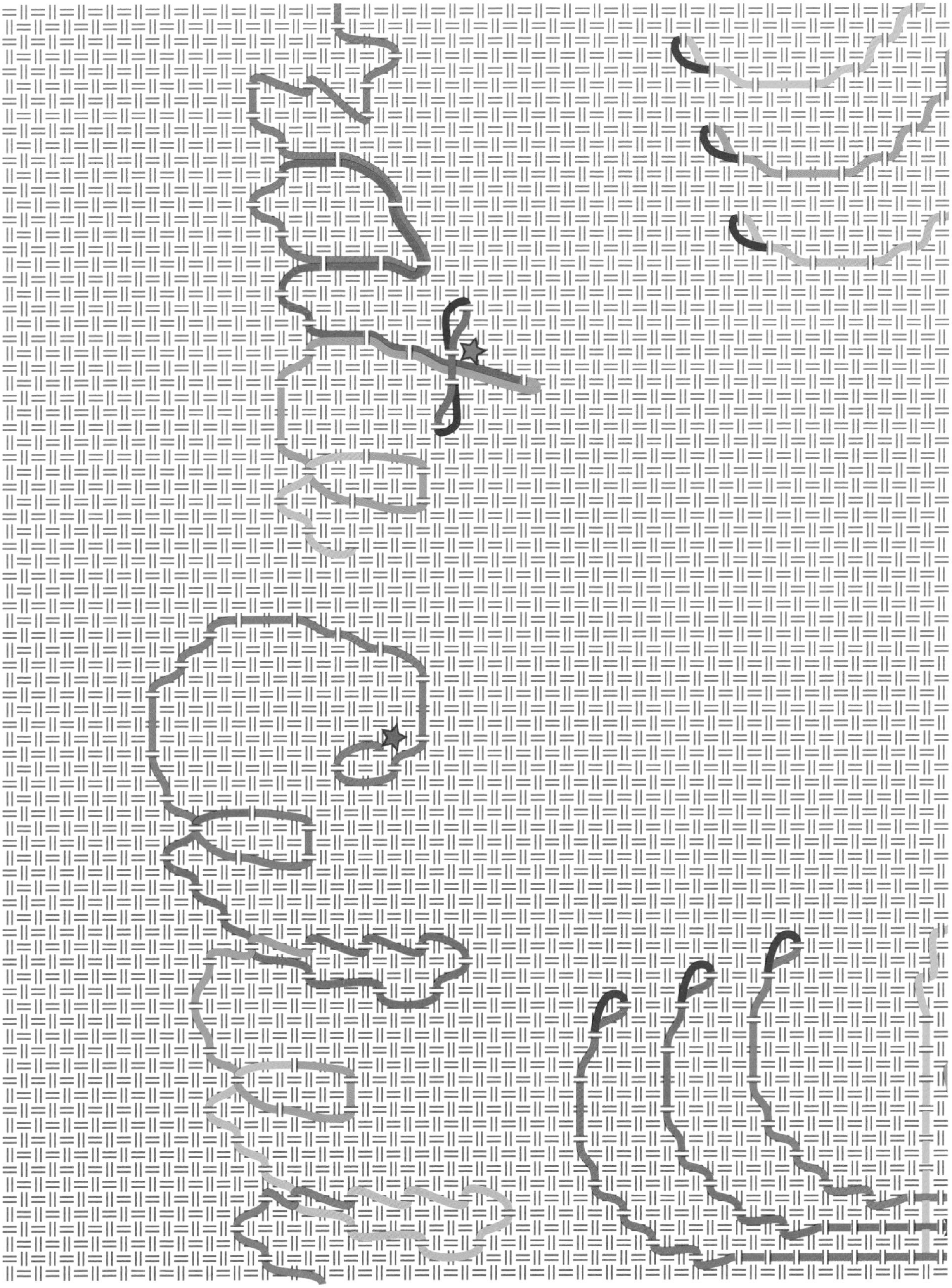

Fireworks Celebration
Chart C

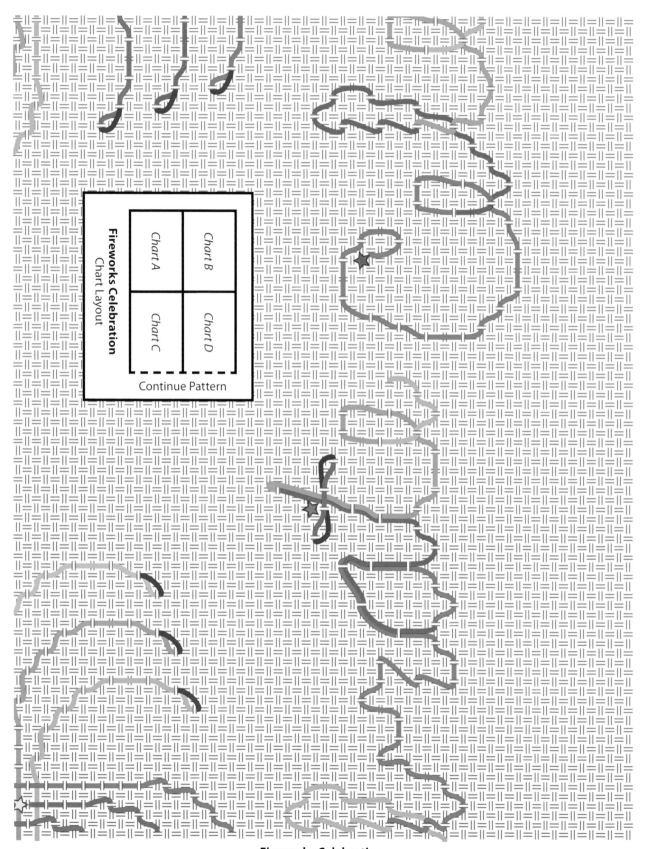

Fireworks Celebration
Chart Layout

| Chart B | Chart A |
| Chart D | Chart C |

Continue Pattern

Fireworks Celebration
Chart D

House of White Birches, Berne, Indiana 46711   AnniesAttic.com

Pine Needles Place Mat
& Napkin Ring

Design by Jeanne Tams

Skill Level

EASY

Finished Sizes
Place Mat: 15½ inches x 18½ inches, including fringe

Napkin Ring: 4½ inches x 8 inches

Materials
- Monk's cloth:
  ⅝ yd natural
- Red Heart Super Saver medium
  (7 oz/364 yds/198g per skein):
  1 skein each #633 dark sage, #661 frosty green,
  #631 light sage and #319 cherry red
- Tapestry needle

Pattern Note
Star marks beginning of stitching.

Instructions

Napkin Ring
Yarn Length & Color
Row 1: 1¾ L + 8 inches dark sage

Row 2: 1¾ L + 8 inches frosty green

Row 3: 3½ L + 8 inches light sage

Row 4: 4 L + 8 inches frosty green

Row 5: 4 L + 8 inches dark sage

Place Mat
Yarn Length & Color
Rows 1, 7 and 8: 1¾ L + 8 inches cherry red

Row 2: 1¾ L + 8 inches dark sage

Row 3: 3½ L + 8 inches frosty green

Row 4: 4 L + 8 inches light sage

Row 5: 4 L + 8 inches frosty green

Row 6: 3½ L + 8 inches dark sage

Finishing
Stay stitch ½-inch from top and bottom edges and along side seams of Napkin Ring. Remove threads to form fringe on long sides. Sew short ends tog with a ⅝-inch seam. ❖

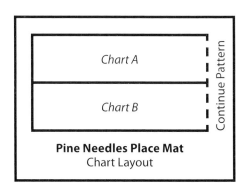

Pine Needles Place Mat
Chart Layout

Chart A

Chart B

Continue Pattern

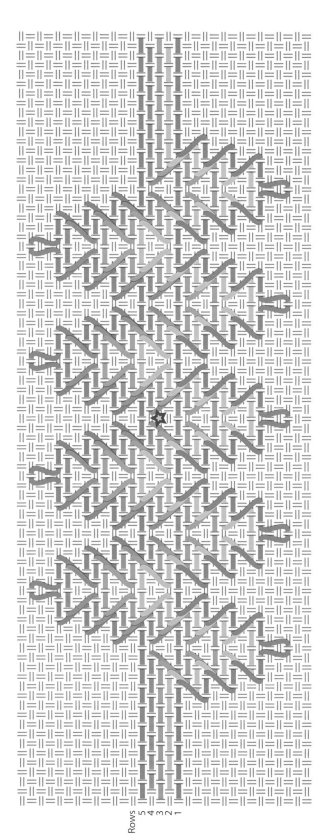

Rows 5 4 3 2 1

Pine Needles Napkin Ring
Chart

House of White Birches, Berne, Indiana 46711   AnniesAttic.com

**Pine Needles
Place Mat**
Chart A

Rows

8
7
6
5
4
3
2
1

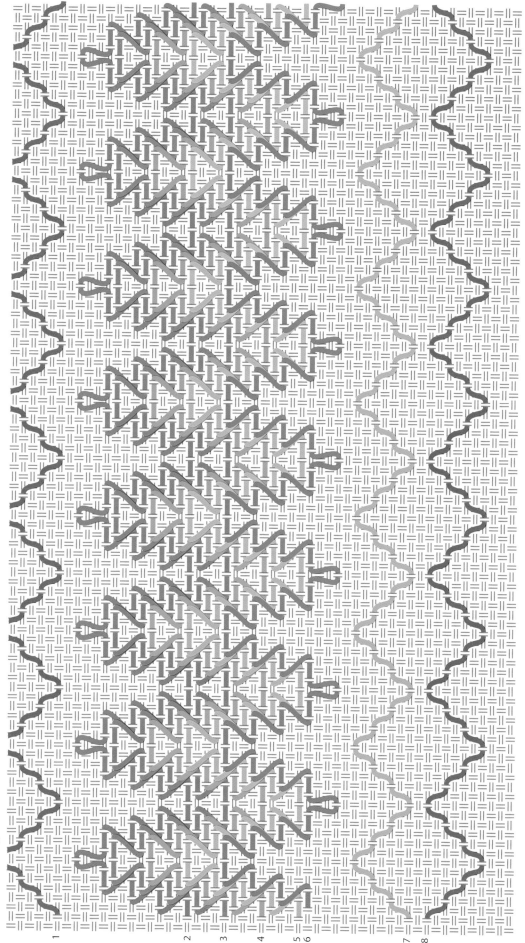

**Pine Needles
Place Mat**
Chart B

Chart Layout

Chart A	
Chart B	Continue Pattern
Chart C	

Pumpkin Patch Table Runner
Chart Layout

Pumpkin Patch
Table Runner

Design by Jeanne Tams

Skill Level

EASY

Finished Size
20 inches x 48 inches

Materials
- Monk's cloth:
  ⅔ yd natural
- Red Heart Super Saver medium
  (7 oz/364 yds/198g per skein):
  1 skein each #254 pumpkin, #633 dark sage,
  #365 coffee, #360 café, #336 warm brown,
  #334 buff, #322 pale yellow and #321 gold
- Tapestry needle

Pattern Notes
The stem with vine is added after pumpkin is finished. The stem with vine row uses loop stitch. Secure yarn ends on back of fabric or retrace 6–8 floats on front side and clip.

Be careful not to pull yarn too tight. Keep each stitch same length as fabric below it.

Star marks beginning of stitching.

The chart colors are not the colors used in the projects.

Instructions
Yarn Length & Color

Rows 1–3, 18 & 19: 1½ L + 8 inches coffee

Rows 4, 17, 20: 1¼ L + 8 inches warm brown

Rows 5, 16, 21: 1¼ L + 8 inches buff

Rows 6, 15, 22: 1¼ L + 8 inches pale yellow

Rows 7, 14, 23: 1¼ L + 8 inches gold

Rows 8, 13, 24: 1¼ L + 8 inches pumpkin

Rows 9, 12: 1¼ L + 8 inches dark sage

Rows 10 & 11: 1¾ L + 8 inches pumpkin

Stem row with vine: 12 inches ❖

**Pumpkin Patch
Table Runner**
Chart A

Rows

24 23 22 21 20 19 18 17 16 15 14 13 12 11, 10

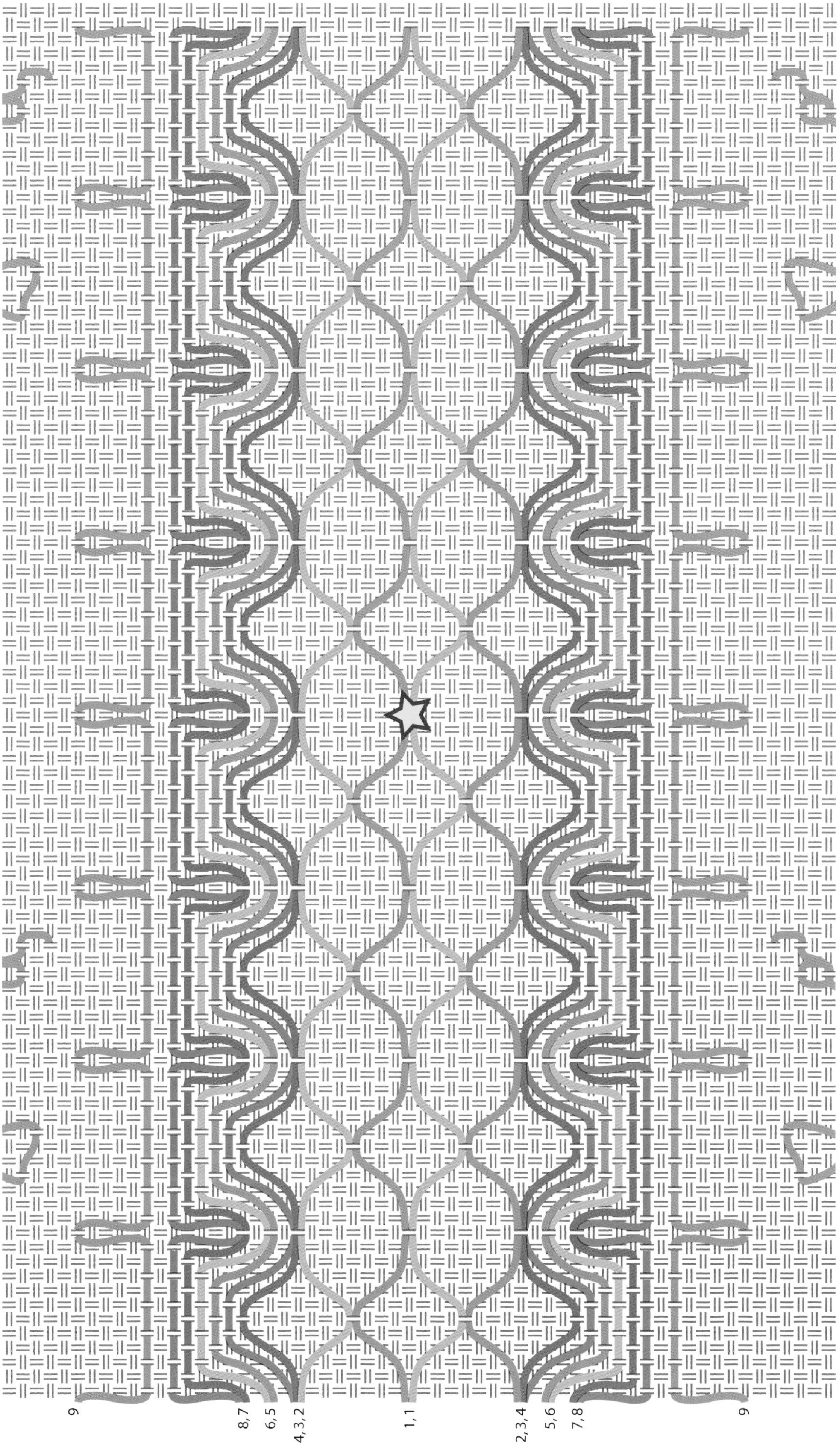

**Pumpkin Patch
Table Runner**
Chart B

9   8,7   6,5   4,3,2   1,1   2,3,4   5,6   7,8   9

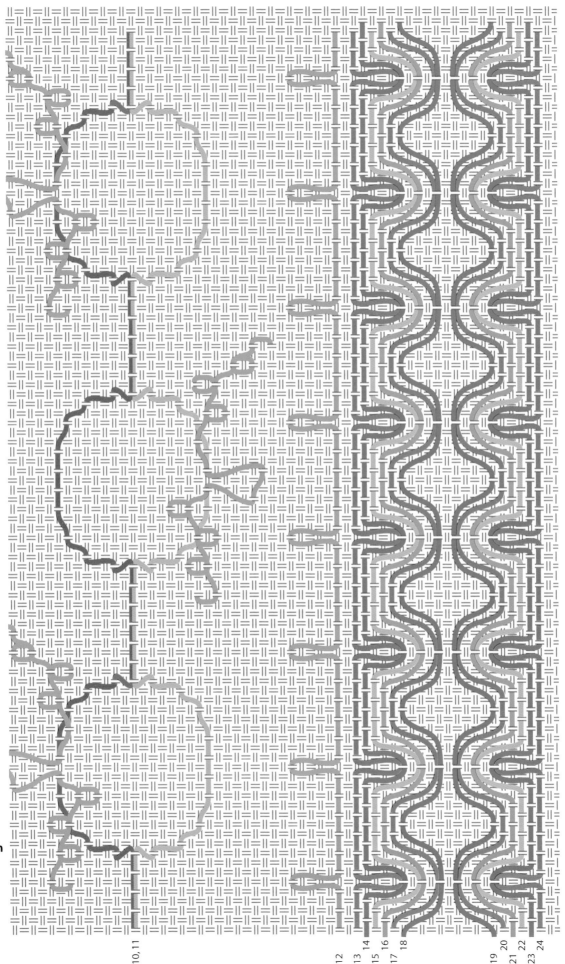

**Pumpkin Patch
Table Runner**
Chart C

10, 11

12

13 14
15
16
17
18

19 20
21 22
23 24

Christmas Table Runner

Design by Jeanne Tams

Skill Level

EASY

Finished Size
23½ inches x 48 inches, including fringe

Materials
- Monk's cloth:
    ¾ yd natural
- Medium (worsted) weight yarn:
    3 oz/150 yds/84g each dark green,
    medium green, light green, burgundy,
    red, gold and yellow
- Tapestry needle

4 MEDIUM

Pattern Notes
Entire stitching pattern is not shown on chart;
repeat pattern across table runner.

Star on chart indicates where to begin stitching.

Instructions
Yarn Length & Color
Row 1: 2 L + 8 inches dark green

Row 2: 2 L + 8 inches medium green

Row 3: 2 L + 8 inches light green

Row 4: ¼ L + 8 inches light green

Row 5: ½ L + 8 inches medium green

Row 6: ½ L + 8 inches dark green

Rows 7, 13: L + 8 inches burgundy

Rows 8, 12: L + 8 inches red

Rows 9, 11: L + 8 inches gold

Row 10: L + 8 inches yellow

Rows 14, 16: 2 L + 8 inches red

Row 15: 2 L + 8 inches burgundy ❖

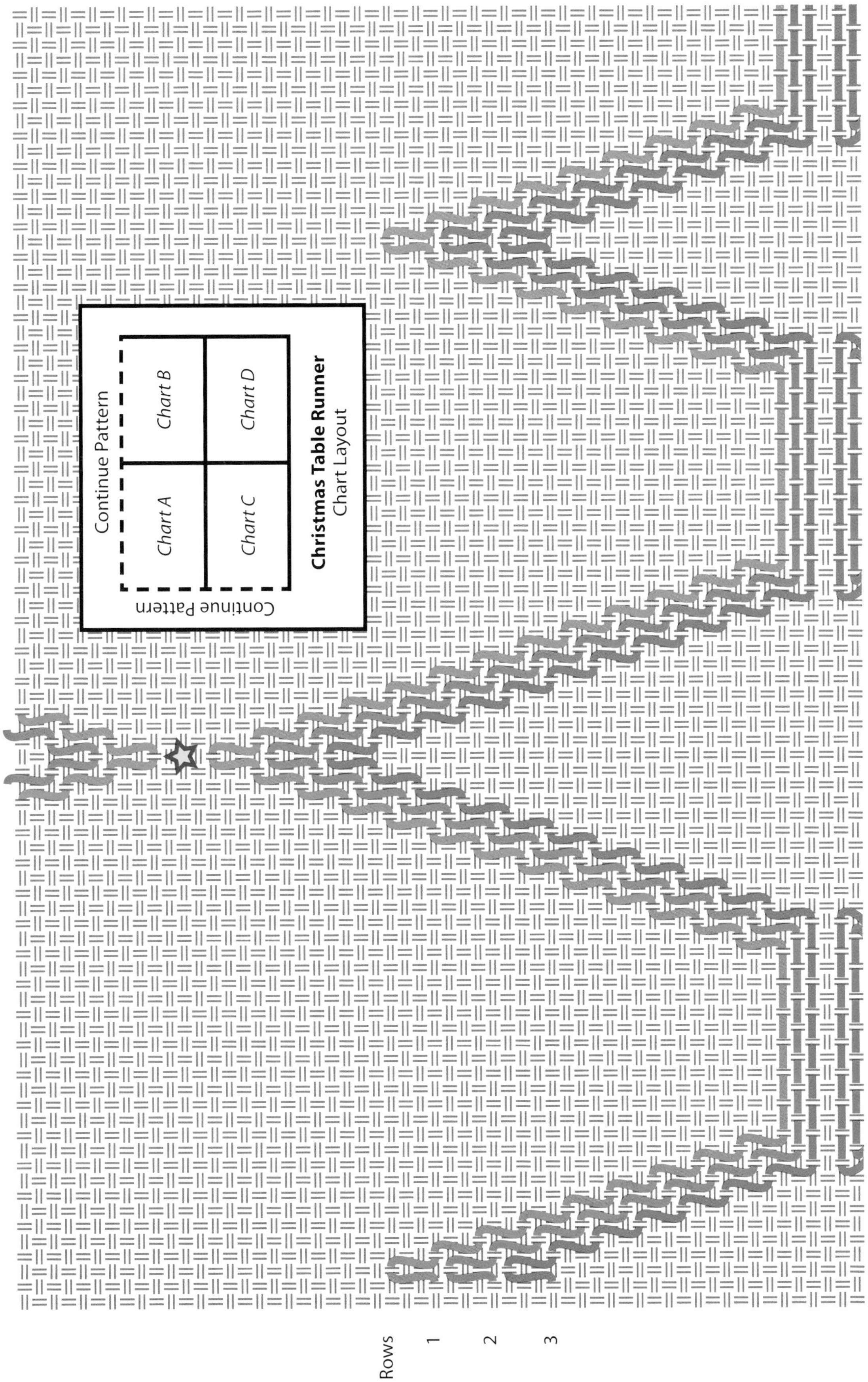

Christmas Table Runner

Chart Layout

Continue Pattern

Chart A	Chart B
Chart C	Chart D

Continue Pattern

Rows

1

2

3

Christmas Table Runner

Chart A

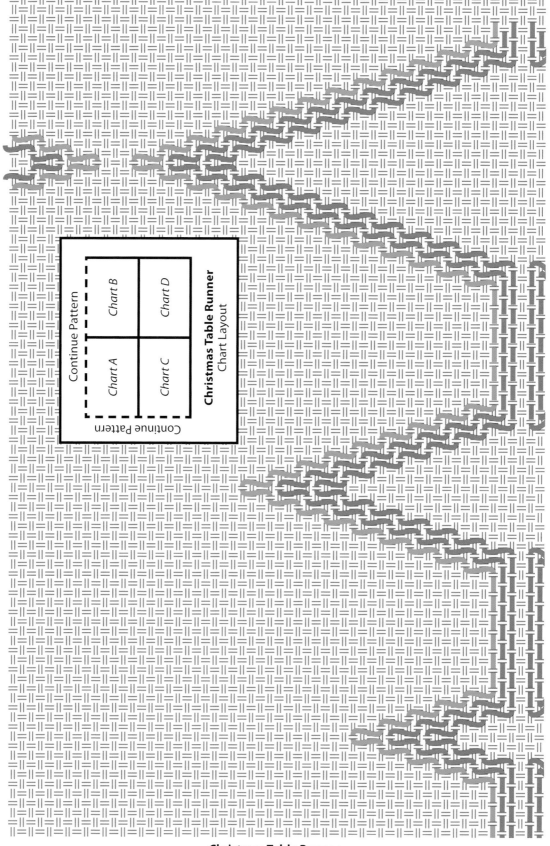

Christmas Table Runner
Chart B

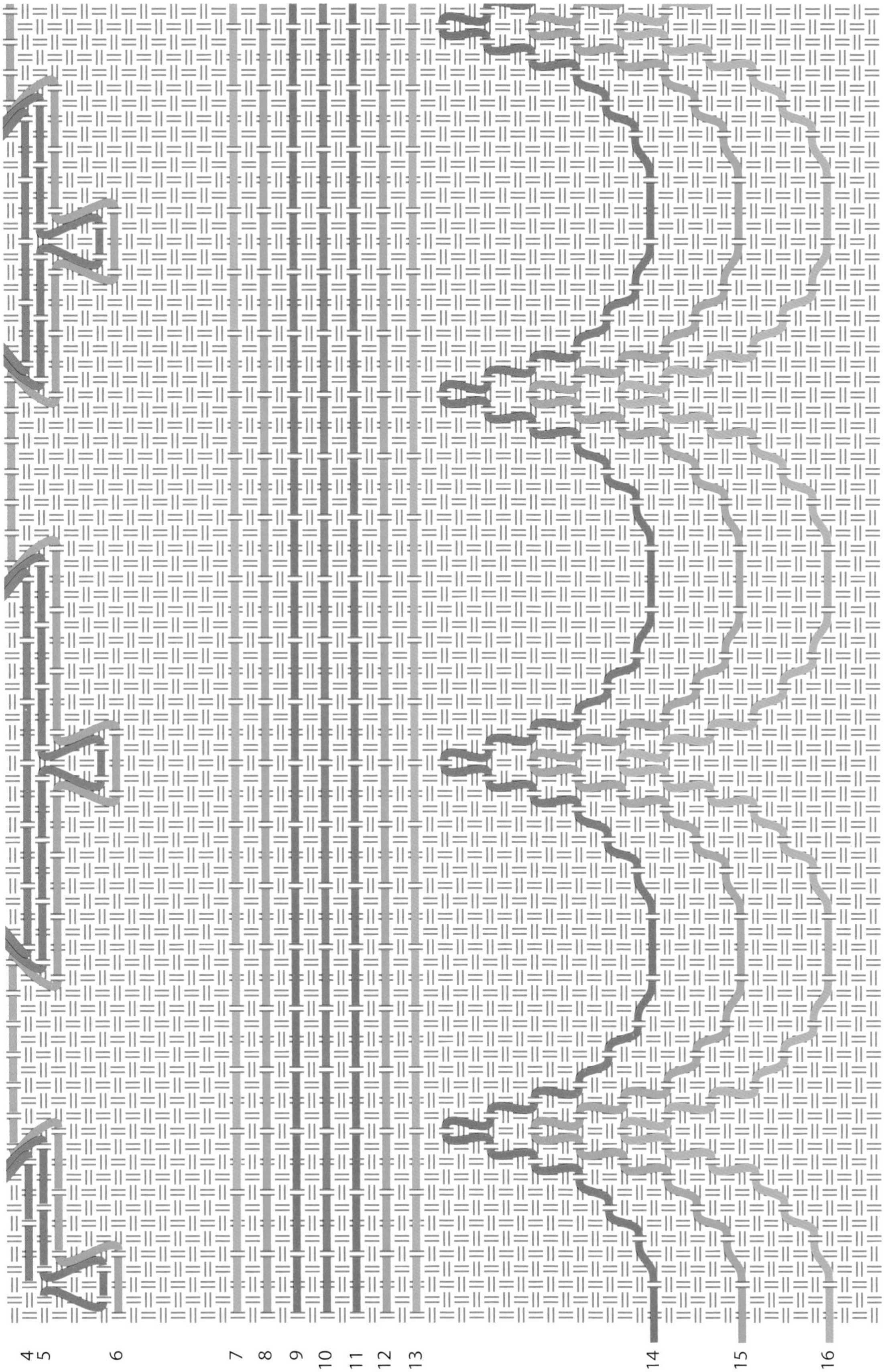

Christmas Table Runner
Chart C

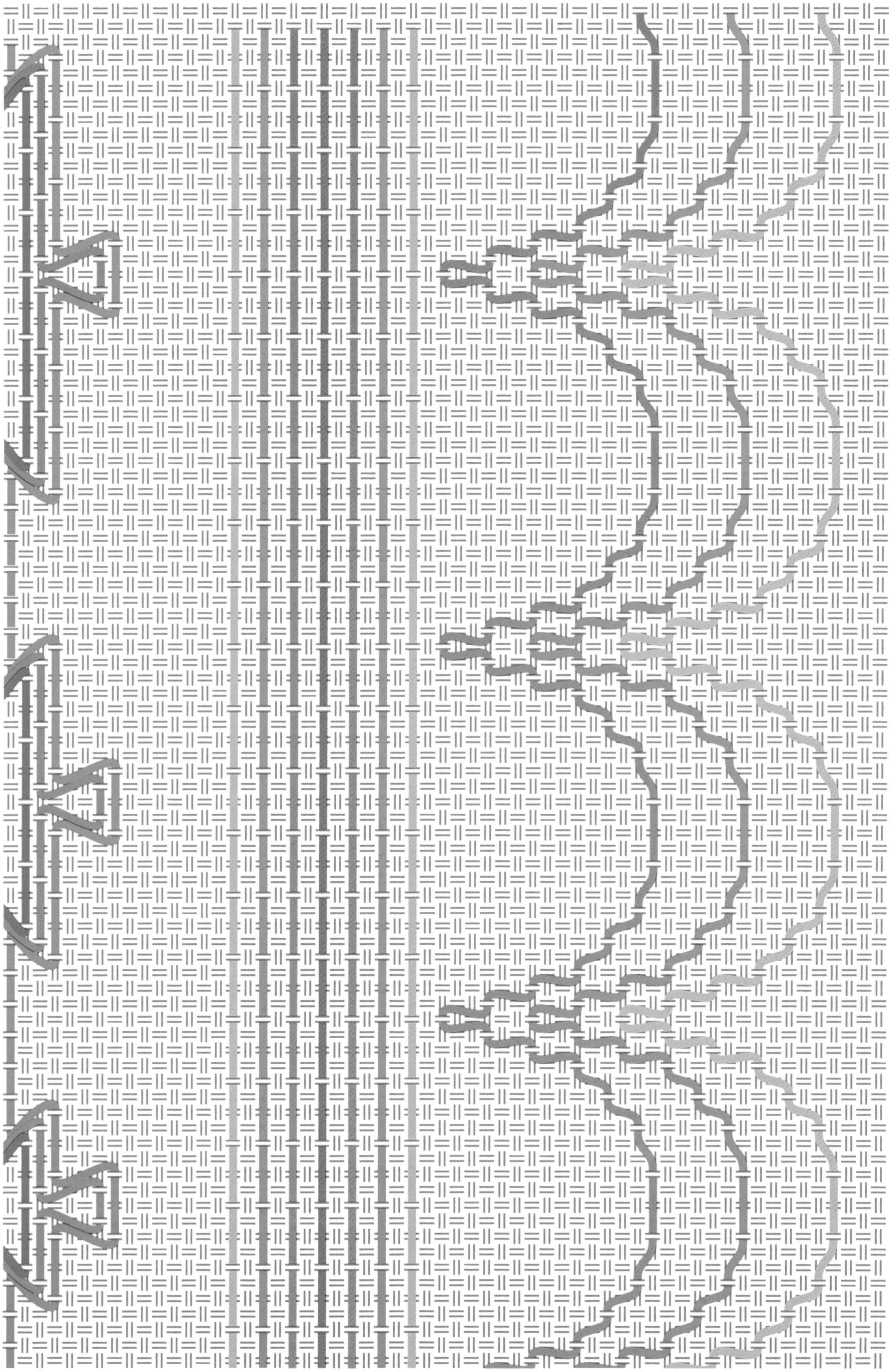

Christmas Table Runner
Chart D

Chart A | Chart B | Continue Pattern

Sand Dunes Pillow
Chart Layout

Sand Dunes Pillow

Design by Jeanne Tams

Skill Level

EASY

Finished Size
17 inches x 17 inches, including fringe

Materials
- Monk's cloth:
  ¾ yd natural
- Lining fabric:
  ½ yd calico
- Red Heart Super Saver medium (worsted) weight yarn (7 oz/364 yds/198g per skein):
  1 skein each #365 coffee, #360 café, #336 warm brown and #334 buff
- Tapestry needle
- 16-inch pillow form

4 MEDIUM

Pattern Note
The chart colors are not the colors used in the projects.

Instructions
Yarn Length & Color

Rows 1, 9 & 10: 6 L + 8 inches coffee

Rows 2, 8: 6¾ L + 8 inches cafe

Rows 3, 7: 6¾ L + 8 inches warm brown

Rows 4, 6: 6¾ L + 8 inches buff

Row 5: 1¾ L + 8 inches coffee

Finishing
Stay stitch around all 4 edges of pillow top. Cut lining fabric same size as pillow top including fringe. Fold over edges of lining fabric, making it same size as pillow top without fringe. Press lining. Pin pillow top to lining fabric with WS tog. Sew 3 sides. Insert pillow form and sew last side. ❖

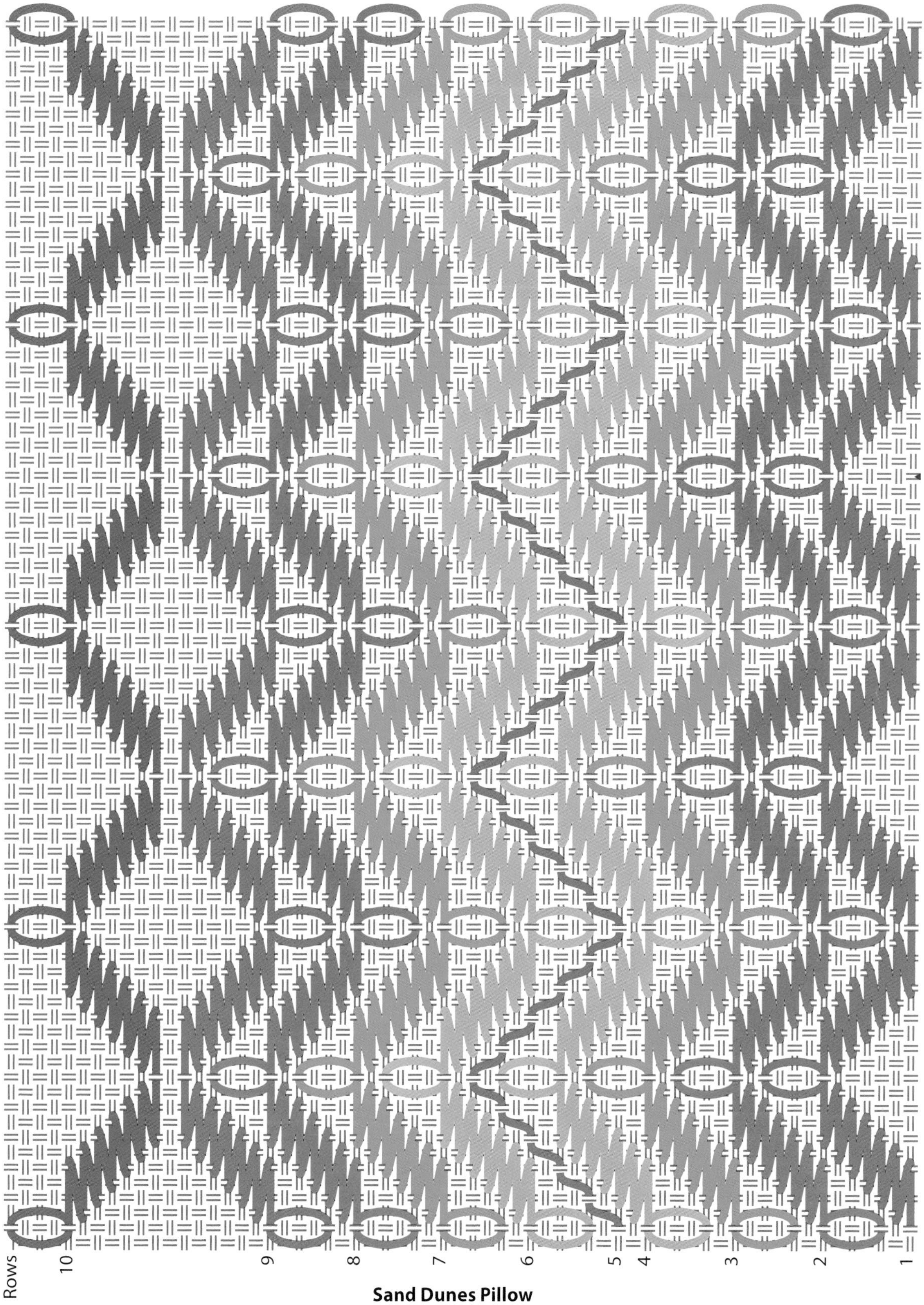

Rows

10

9

8

7

6

5

4

3

2

1

Sand Dunes Pillow
Chart A

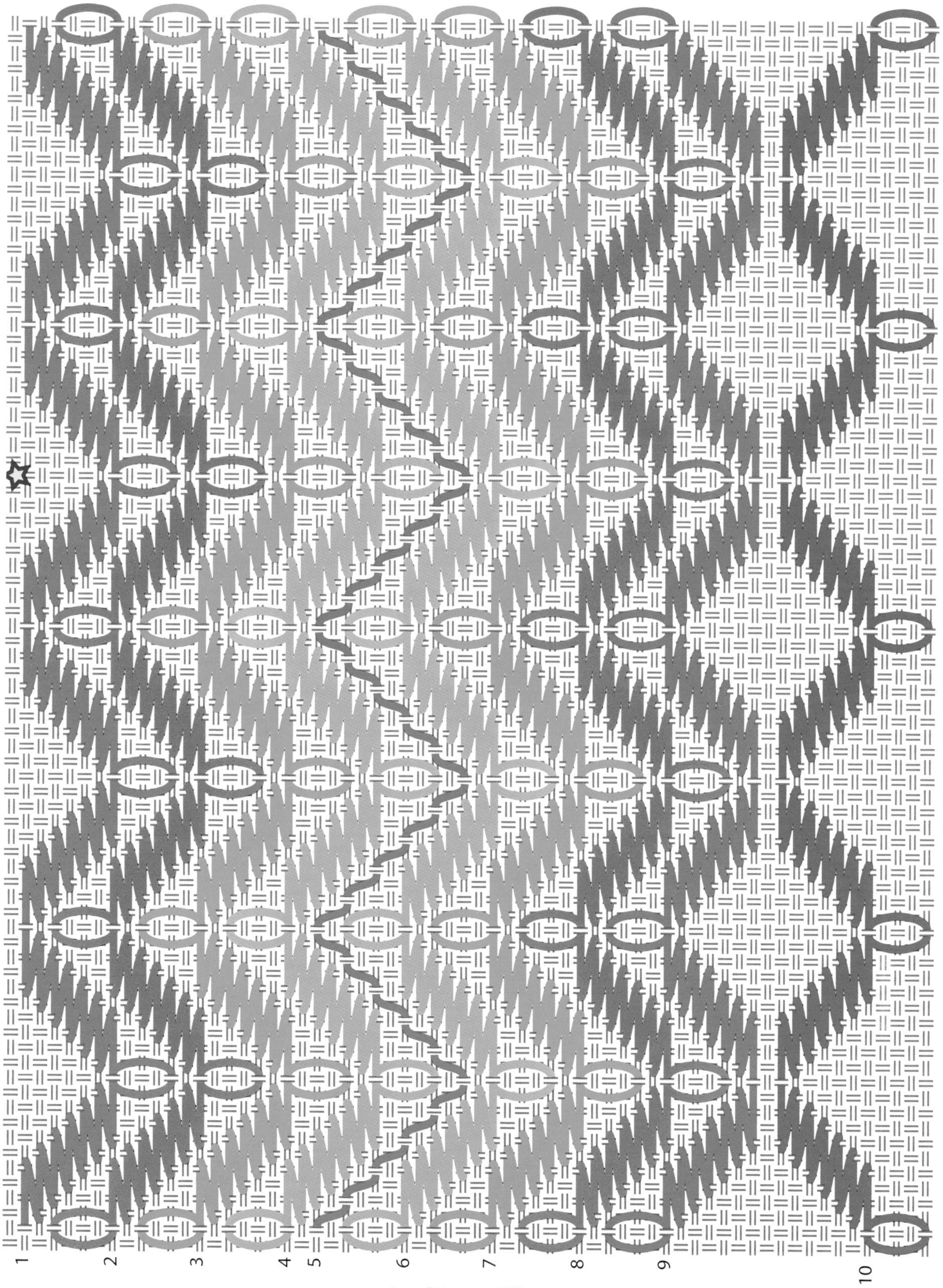

Sand Dunes Pillow
Chart B

House of White Birches, Berne, Indiana 46711   AnniesAttic.com

Marquis Pillow

Design by Jeanne Tams

Skill Level

EASY

Finished Size

16½ inches x 16½ inches, including fringe

Materials

- Monk's cloth:
  ⅝ yd natural
- Lining fabric:
  ½ yd calico
- Medium (worsted) weight yarn:
  3 oz/150 yds/84g each dark blue, medium blue, blue and burgundy
- Tapestry needle
- 16-inch pillow form

4 MEDIUM

Instructions

Yarn Length & Color

Rows 1, 9: 2 L + 8 inches burgundy

Rows 2, 8, 10: 2 L + 8 inches blue

Rows 3, 7, 11: 2 L + 8 inches medium blue

Rows 4, 6, 12: ½ L + 8 inches dark blue

Rows 5, 13: 3 L + 8 inches burgundy

Finishing

Stay stitch around all four edges of the pillow top. Cut lining fabric same size as pillow top including fringe. Fold over edges of lining, making it same size as pillow top without fringe. Press lining. Pin pillow top to lining with WS tog. Sew 3 sides. Insert pillow form and sew last side. ❖

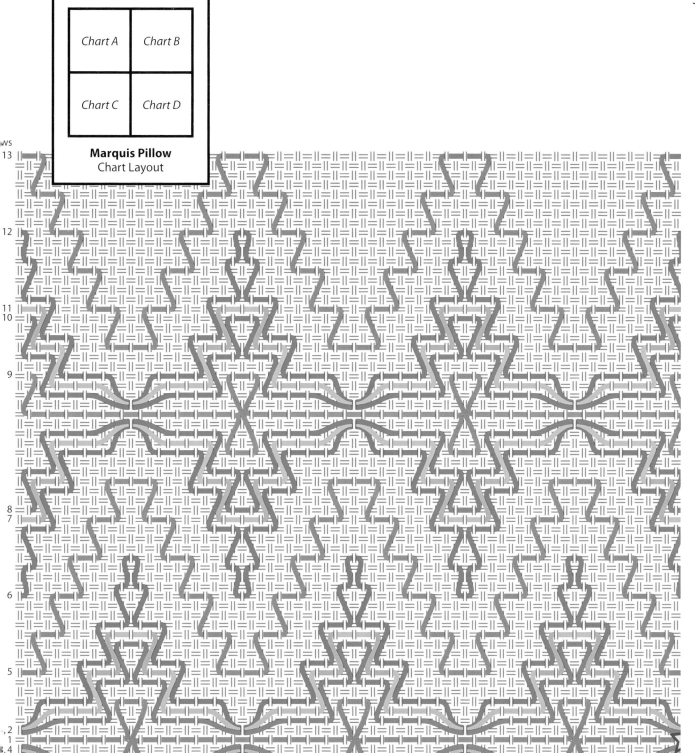

Marquis Pillow
Chart Layout

Marquis Pillow
Chart A

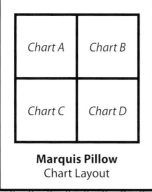

Marquis Pillow
Chart Layout

Marquis Pillow
Chart B

Marquis Pillow
Chart C

Marquis Pillow
Chart D

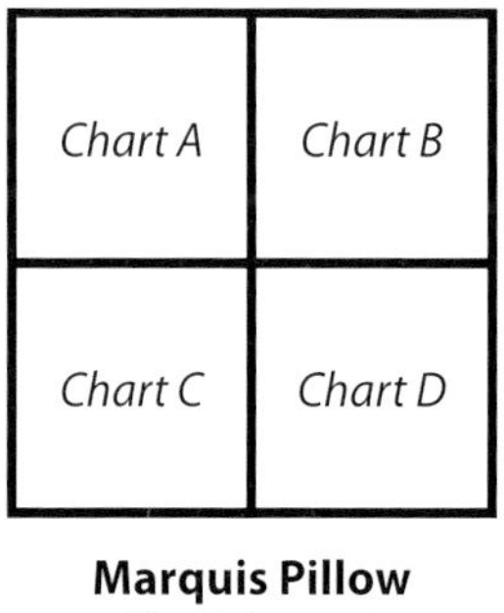

Chart A	Chart B
Chart C	Chart D

Marquis Pillow
Chart Layout

Seashells Scissors Case

Design by Jeanne Tams

Skill Level

EASY

Finished Size
10 inches x 8 inches

Materials
• Monk's cloth:
  ½ yd natural
• Lining fabric:
  ⅓ yd calico

• Red Heart Super Saver medium
  (7 oz/364 yds/198g per skein):
    1 skein each #374 country rose and
    #387 soft navy
• Red Heart Classic medium
  (3½ oz/190 yds/99g per skein):
    1 skein each #762 claret and #755 pale rose
• Tapestry needle
• Sewing needle
• ¾-inch pink button
• Matching sewing thread

56

Pattern Note

The chart colors are not the colors used in the projects.

Instructions

Yarn Length & Color

Rows 1, 22: 1¼ L + 8 inches navy

Rows 2–5, 18–21: 2¼ L + 8 inches pale rose

Rows 6–9, 14–17: 2¼ L + 8 inches country rose

Rows 10–13: 2¼ L + 8 inches claret

Row 23: 2¼ L + 8 inches navy

Finishing

Stay stitch around all 4 edges of the scissors case. Cut lining fabric same size as scissors case including fringe. Fold over edges of lining, making it same size as scissors case without fringe. Press lining. Pin scissors case to lining with WS tog. Sew sides. Referring to photo, overlap corners and sew button to secure overlap. ❖

The red line is the cutting line. The blue line is the stitching line. The purple lines are the fold lines. The star is the center point. The circle is for button placement.

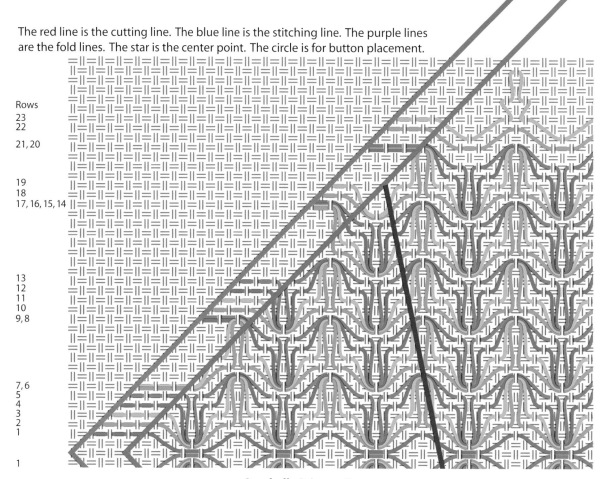

Rows
23
22
21, 20
19
18
17, 16, 15, 14
13
12
11
10
9, 8
7, 6
5
4
3
2
1
1

Seashells Scissors Case
Chart A

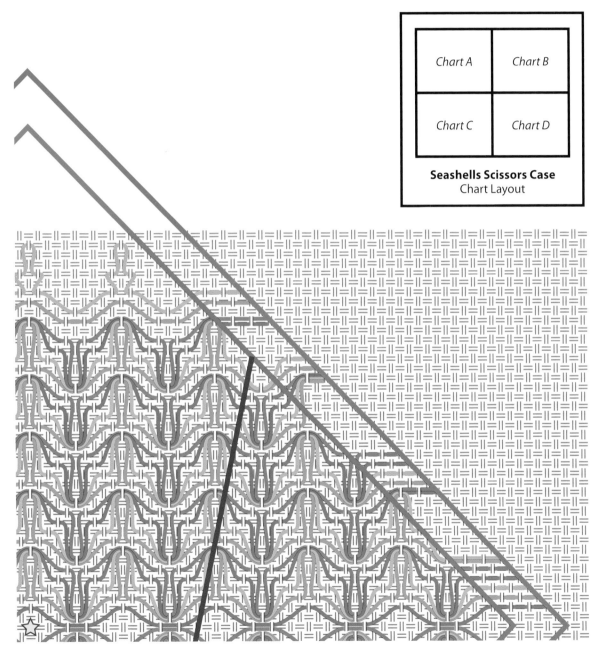

Seashells Scissors Case
Chart B

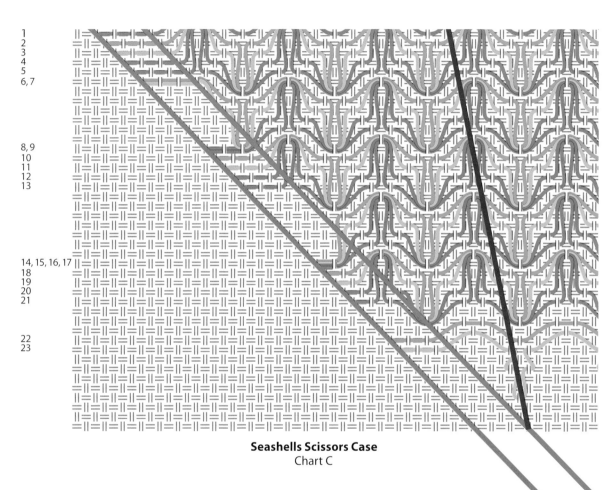

1
2
3
4
5
6, 7

8, 9
10
11
12
13

14, 15, 16, 17
18
19
20
21

22
23

Seashells Scissors Case
Chart C

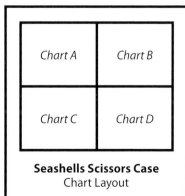

| Chart A | Chart B |
| Chart C | Chart D |

Seashells Scissors Case
Chart Layout

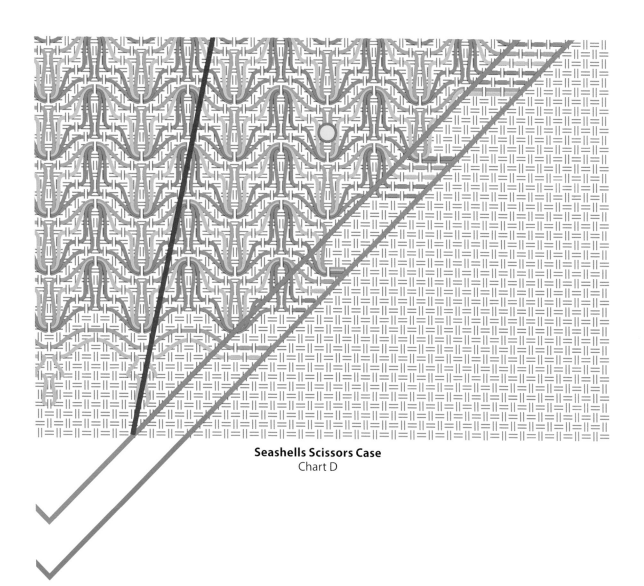

Seashells Scissors Case
Chart D

Blossoms Pincushion

Design by Jeanne Tams

Skill Level

EASY

Finished Size

8 inches x 8 inches, including fringe

Materials

- Monk's cloth:
  ¼ yd natural
- Red Heart Classic medium
  (3½ oz/190 yds/99g per skein):
  1 skein each #815 pale blue, #631 light sage,
  #737 pink and #261 maize
- Tapestry needle
- ⅜-inch blue button
- 8 inches x 8 inches piece of felt
- Polyester fiberfill

4 MEDIUM

Pattern Notes

Begin stitching diagonal rows with blossoms using rotating loop stitch according to chart. Then stitch other diagonals. At blossom center, repeat center stitch, looping 2nd stitch over top of blossom.

Some chart colors do not match the colors used in the project.

In chart, if row numbers appear at only one row end, begin row at numbered end. If numbers appear at both row ends, begin row at either end.

Instructions

Yarn Length & Color
Row 1: 30 inches pink

Rows 2 & 3: 23 inches pale blue

Rows 4 & 5: 16 inches pink

Row 6: 16 inches light sage

Rows 7 & 8: 13 inches maize

Rows 9 & 10: 10 inches light sage

Finishing

Stay stitch around all 4 edges of pincushion. Cut felt same size as pincushion without fringe. Pin pincushion to felt lining with WS tog. Sew around 3 sides. Insert polyester fiberfill. Sew last side. Sew button in center of pincushion through all layers. ❖

Right Hand   The red line is the cutting line. The blue line is the stitching line.

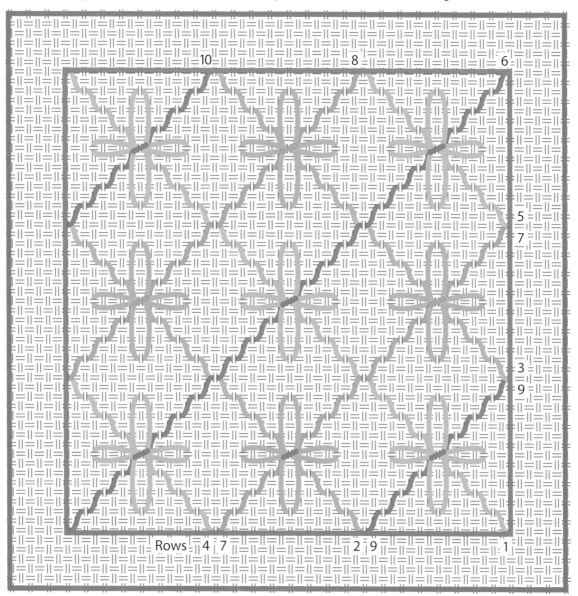

Blossoms Pincushion
Chart A

House of White Birches, Berne, Indiana 46711   AnniesAttic.com

Left Hand   The red line is the cutting line. The blue line is the stitching line.

Blossoms Pincushion
Chart B

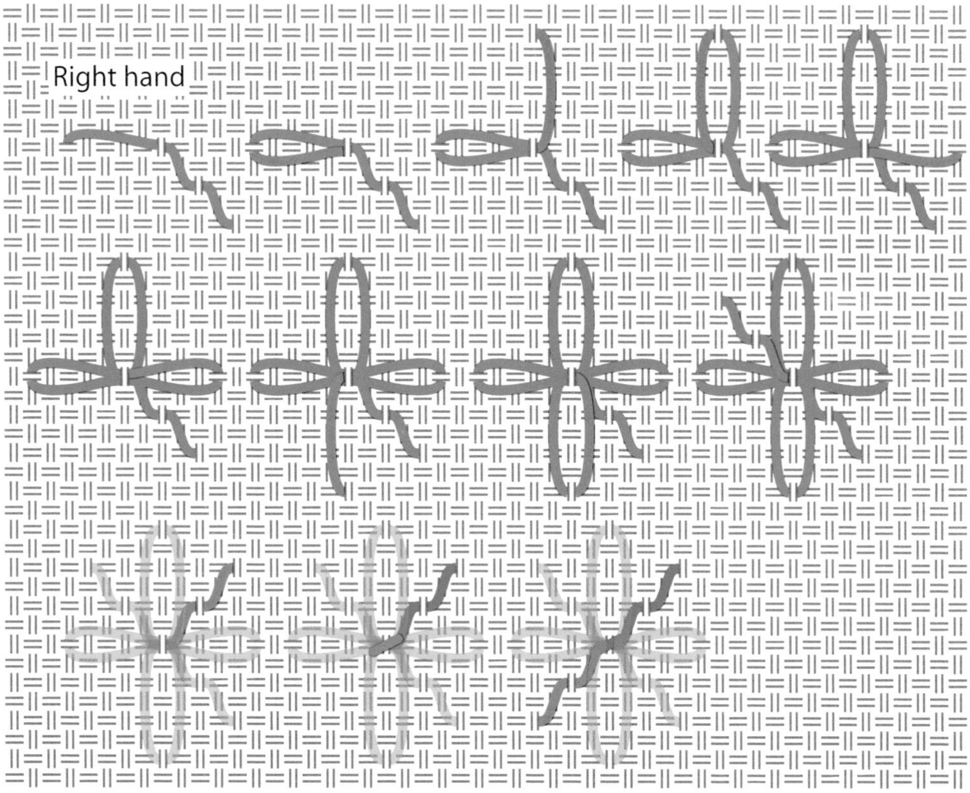

Right hand

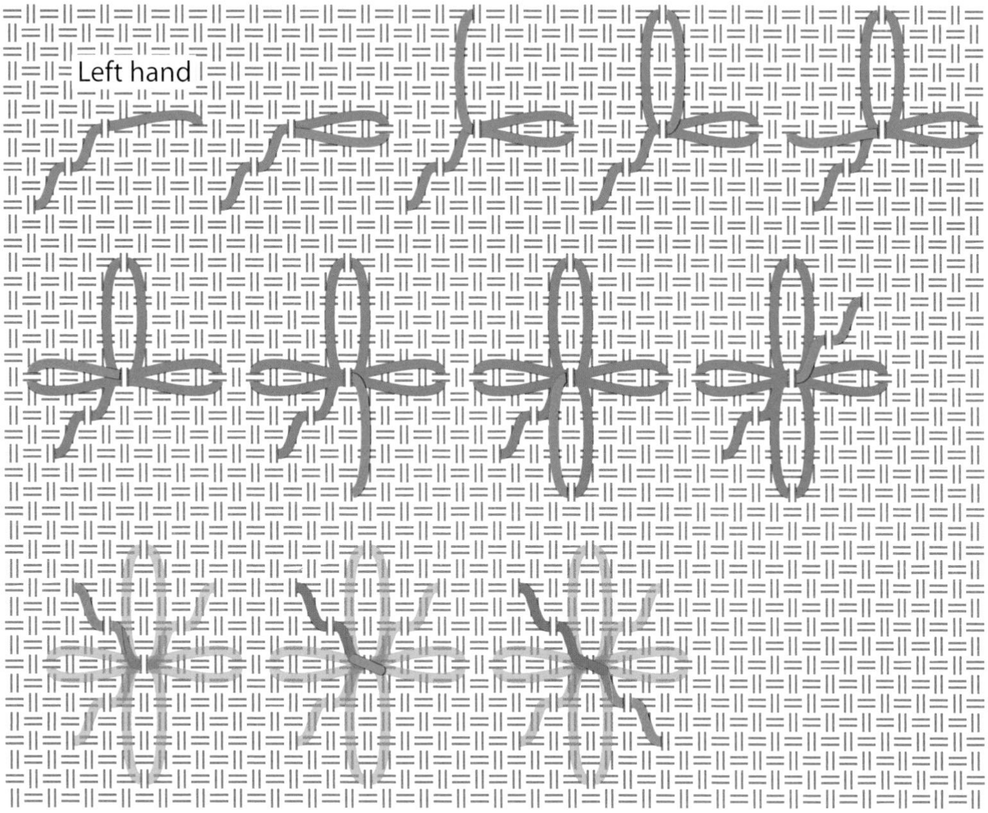

Left hand

Photo Index

HOUSE of
WHITE
BIRCHES
PUBLISHERS
SINCE 1947

Monk's Cloth: 17 Fun & Easy Projects is published by DRG, 306 East Parr Road, Berne, IN 46711. Printed in USA. Copyright © 2010 DRG. All rights reserved. This publication may not be reproduced in part or in whole without written permission from the publisher.

RETAIL STORES: If you would like to carry this pattern book or any other DRG publications, visit DRGwholesale.com

Every effort has been made to ensure that the instructions in this publication are complete and accurate. We cannot, however, take responsibility for human error, typographical mistakes or variations in individual work. Please visit AnniesCustomerCare.com to check for pattern updates.

ISBN: 978-1-59217-297-9

3 4 5 6 7 8 9